MULTICULTURAL SEASONAL CRAFTS

SUMMER CRAFTS FROM DIFFERENT CULTURES

12 Projects to Celebrate the Season

BY MEGAN BORGERT-SPANIOL

Raintree is an imprint of Capstone Global Library Limited, a company incorporated in England and Wales having its registered office at 264 Banbury Road, Oxford, OX2 7DY – Registered company number: 6695582

www.raintree.co.uk
myorders@raintree.co.uk

Hardback edition © Capstone Global Library Limited 2023
Paperback edition © Capstone Global Library Limited 2024

The moral rights of the proprietor have been asserted. All rights reserved. No part of this publication may be reproduced in any form or by any means (including photocopying or storing it in any medium by electronic means and whether or not transiently or incidentally to some other use of this publication) without the written permission of the copyright owner, except in accordance with the provisions of the Copyright, Designs and Patents Act 1988 or under the terms of a licence issued by the Copyright Licensing Agency, 5th Floor, Shackleton House, 4 Battle Bridge Lane, London, SE1 2HX (www.cla.co.uk). Applications for the copyright owner's written permission should be addressed to the publisher.

British Library Cataloguing in Publication Data
A full catalogue record for this book is available from the British Library.

ISBN 978 1 3982 4546 4 (hardback)
ISBN 978 1 3982 4545 7 (paperback)

Editorial Credits
Editor: Jessica Rusick
Designer: Sarah DeYoung
Originated by Capstone Global Library Ltd

Image Credits
Project and materials photos: Mighty Media, Inc.; Shutterstock: Binh Thanh Bui, 5 (crepe paper), Daxiao Productions, 6 (girl), Rido, 10 (photograph)

Design Elements
Shutterstock: KALYA MALYA, lukeruk, sherilhome

All the internet addresses (URLs) given in this book were valid at the time of going to press. However, due to the dynamic nature of the internet, some addresses may have changed, or sites may have changed or ceased to exist since publication. While the author and publisher regret any inconvenience this may cause readers, no responsibility for any such changes can be accepted by either the author or the publisher.

CONTENTS

Summer 4

Seasonal craft 6

Pride Month........................... 8

Father's Day........................... 10

Midsommar............................ 12

Canada Day............................ 14

Fourth of July 16

Bastille Day 18

Nelson Mandela International Day........ 20

International Day of Friendship.......... 22

Lughnasadh............................ 24

Hungry Ghost Festival................ 26

Juneteenth 28

   Find out more....................... 32

   About the author................... 32

Summer

What is your favourite part of summer? Is it the stylish sunglasses or ice-cold treats? Maybe it's all the seasonal celebrations, including Father's Day and the International Day of Friendship!

Celebrate summer with cool projects that reflect the season. Create a Canada Day windsock or some Bastille Day fireworks. You can even make rainbow shoelaces for Pride Month or an orange slice garland for the Hungry Ghost Festival. Summer is filled with enough natural beauty and festivities to keep you crafting all season long!

BASIC SUPPLIES

craft glue

craft tape

crepe paper

hot glue gun

paint and paintbrushes

push pins

ribbon

ruler

scissors

string

CRAFTING TIPS

Be prepared! Read through the materials and instructions before starting a project. Cover your workspace with paper or plastic to protect it from messes or spills.

Think outside the book! Lots of the projects in this book use materials you'll probably find around your home. Is there something you can't find? Think of ways to adapt the project using items you do have.

Ask first! Get permission before using materials you find at home or school. Also ask before you collect items from nature and bring them indoors.

Be safe! Ask an adult for help with projects that require sharp or hot tools.

Clean up! When your project is complete, put all materials and tools back where you found them. Clean up any spills and wipe down your crafting surface.

SEASONAL CRAFT
Stylish sunglasses

Sunglasses are a summertime must-have. They protect your eyes from harsh sunlight, and they look good while doing it! With a couple of bottles of nail varnish, you can freshen up old frames into a sweet pair of shades. Then go outside – summer awaits!

What you need

- 3 colours of nail varnish
- sunglasses with thick frames
- buttons
- hot glue gun

What you do

1. Choose three colours of nail varnish that look good together.

2. Use one nail varnish colour to paint the top of the sunglasses frames, from one corner across the nose bridge to the other corner. Let the nail varnish dry.

3. Use the second colour to paint the rounded bottom edges of the frames. Let the nail varnish dry.

4. Use the third colour to paint the arms of the sunglasses. Let the nail varnish dry.

5. Hot-glue small buttons to the corners of your sunglasses. Let the glue dry. Then wear your stylish sunglasses outside!

Fun fact

Early sunglasses were crafted by Indigenous Alaskans thousands of years ago. The sunglasses were made of bone, wood and other materials.

PRIDE MONTH
Rainbow shoelaces

Pride is a month-long celebration of the history, contributions and culture of the lesbian, gay, bisexual, transgender and queer (LGBTQ) community. Rainbow flags are a popular symbol of the LGBTQ community. With a few marker pens and some surgical spirit, you can wear your own Pride rainbow on your shoes!

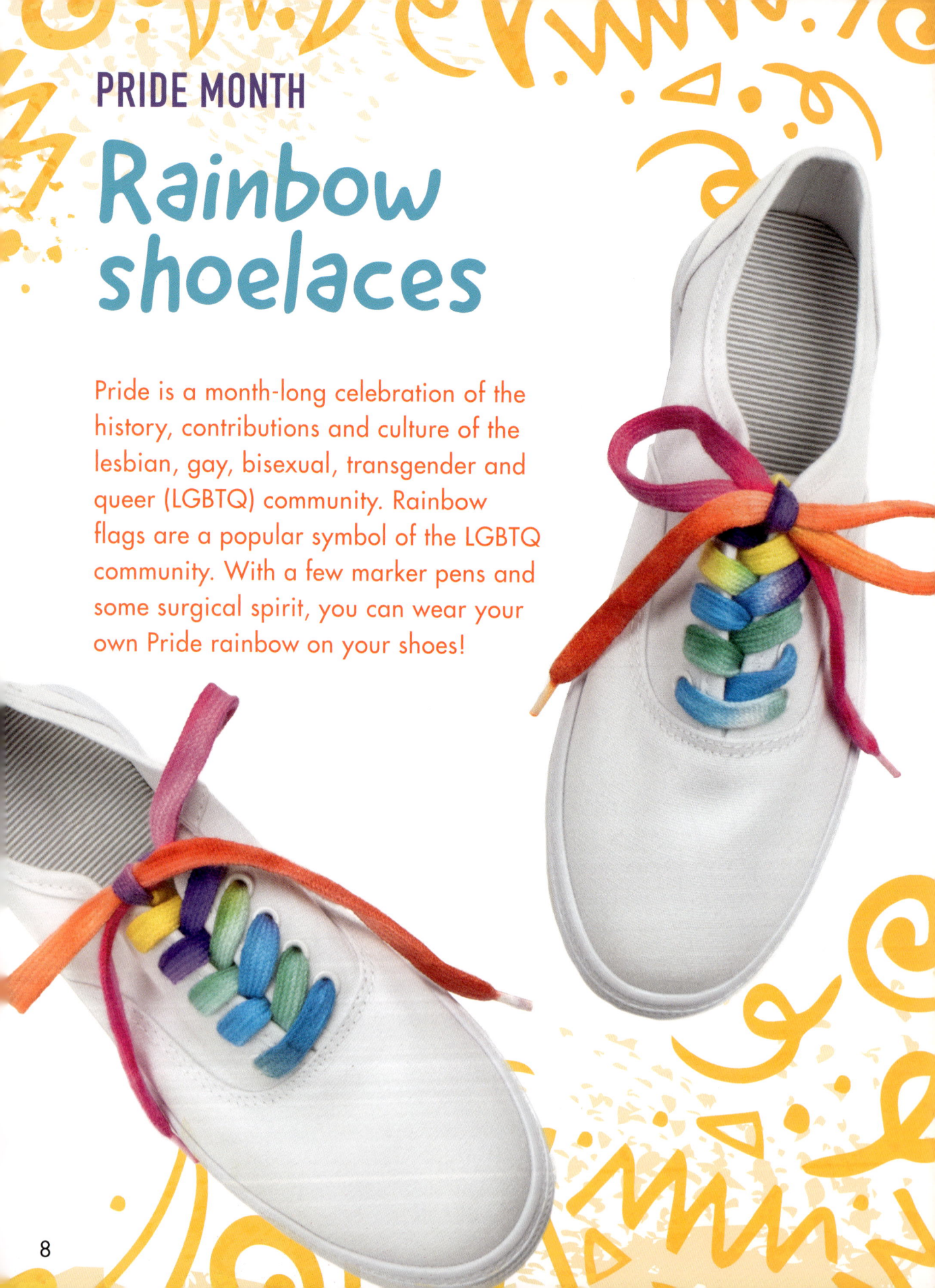

What you need

- white shoelaces
- ruler
- pencil
- plastic for work surface
- permanent markers in rainbow colours
- dropper (pipette)
- surgical spirit

What you do

1. Measure the length of your shoelace. Divide that number by the number of colours you will use. Use a pencil to mark the divisions on the shoelace.

2. Cover your work surface with plastic to protect it. Colour in the first shoelace section with your first colour. Flip the shoelace over to colour the other side of the section. The ink does not have to reach the edges of the shoelace.

3. Repeat step 2 with the remaining colours and shoelace sections.

4. Lay the coloured shoelace flat. Fill a dropper with surgical spirit. Drip the liquid onto the shoelace, one small section at a time. The marker ink will start to bleed. Flip the shoelace over to cover both sides in surgical spirit. Let the shoelace dry.

5. Repeat steps 1 to 4 to colour your other shoelace. Then lace up your shoes and show off your colours!

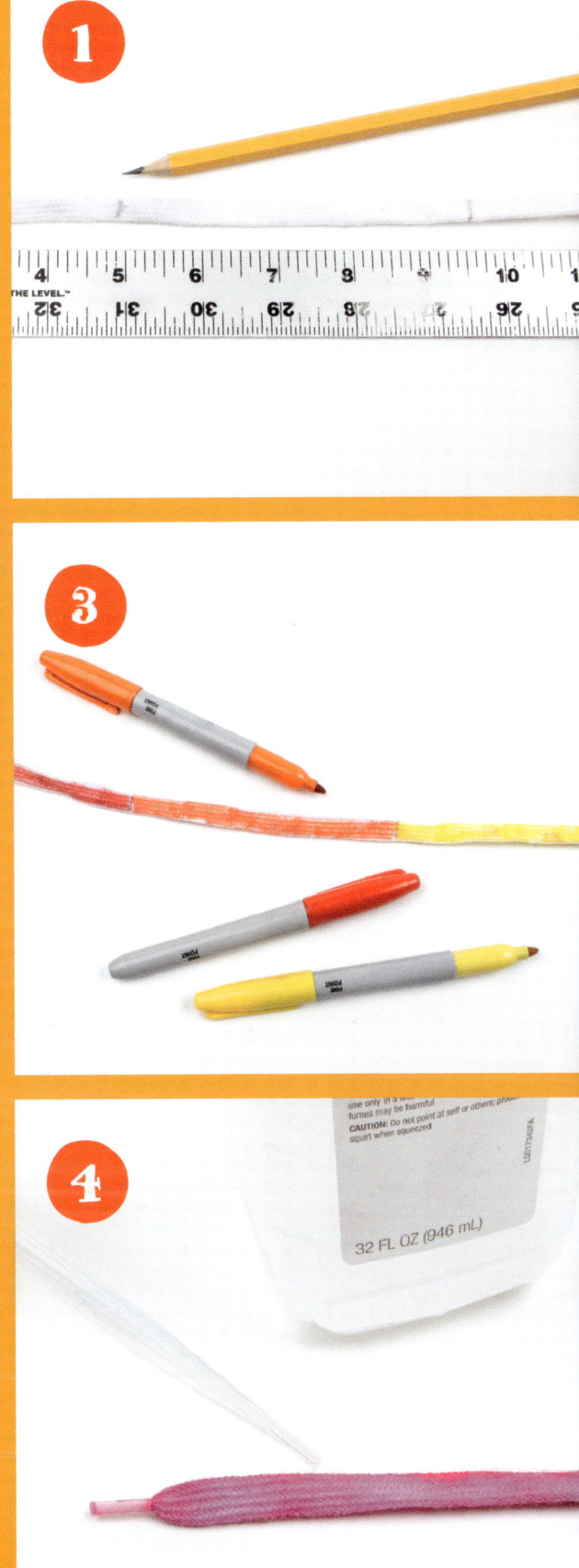

FATHER'S DAY
Bow tie frame

Cultures around the world celebrate fatherhood in different ways. In the UK, people celebrate Father's Day by giving gifts to a father or male caregiver. Show appreciation for someone in your life with a framed photo of the two of you!

What you need

- old magazine
- ruler
- scissors
- hot glue gun
- picture frame
- paint and paintbrush (optional)
- photo

What you do

1. Rip out colourful pages from an old magazine.

2. Cut a strip from one page that is 5 cm (2 in) wide and as long as the length of the page.

3. Accordion-fold the strip along its width. Make the folds every 0.5 cm (¼ in).

4. Cut a strip of magazine paper that is 0.5 × 5 cm (¼ in × 2 in). Glue the strip around the middle of the accordion-folded paper. Fan out the folds on either side to create a bow tie.

5. Repeat steps 2 to 4 to make as many bow ties as you like.

6. If you want, you can paint the picture frame a colour of your choosing. Let the paint dry.

7. Glue the bow ties to the frame in any pattern you like. Then place a photo of you and your father or caregiver in the frame!

MIDSOMMAR

Maypole wand

Midsommar is a Scandinavian festival marking the summer solstice, the longest day of the year. A central part of Midsommar celebrations is the maypole. People sing and dance around this tall pole that is decked in ribbons, flowers and leaves. Make your own personal maypole wand to wave in honour of Midsommar!

Fun fact

In northern parts of Scandinavia, the Sun never fully sets on and around the summer solstice.

What you need

- paint and paintbrush (optional)
- 30.5-cm (12-in) wooden dowel
- ribbon
- ruler
- scissors
- push pin
- fake (or real) flowers, leaves or other bits of summertime nature
- hot glue gun
- puffy paint or glitter glue (optional)

What you do

1. If you like, paint the wooden dowel a colour of your choosing. Let it dry.

2. Cut three lengths of ribbon that are 30.5 to 38 cm (12 to 15 in) each. Use multiple colours of ribbon if you'd like.

3. Find the middle point of each ribbon. Stack the ribbons at their middle points.

4. Place the stacked ribbons over one end of the wooden dowel and secure them with a push pin.

5. Hot glue fake flowers, leaves, or other bits of summertime nature around the push pin. You can use real flowers and greenery too, but they won't last as long.

6. If you like, decorate the dowel with puffy paint or glitter glue.

7. Your wand is complete! Try weaving the ribbons around the wand like it's a maypole. Or let the ribbons fly loose in the summer breeze!

CANADA DAY
Maple leaf windsock

Canada is the second-largest country in the world. It also has the world's longest coastline and about 10 per cent of the world's forests! Canadians around the world celebrate their nation on 1 July. Join the festivities by crafting a windsock inspired by Canada's maple leaf flag!

What you need

- empty tin
- tin opener
- paint (white, red) and paintbrushes
- maple leaf (real or fake)
- clear tape or poster putty
- small paintbrush
- red crepe paper
- ruler
- scissors
- hot glue gun
- string
- tape

What you do

1. Have an adult help you cut out the bottom of an empty tin using a tin opener.

2. Paint the tin white. Let it dry.

3. Remove the stem from the maple leaf. Put clear tape or poster putty on the back of the leaf to lightly secure the leaf to the tin.

4. Dip the small paintbrush in red paint. Paint small brush strokes going outwards from the leaf to outline its shape on the tin.

5. Once the red paint is dry, gently pull the maple leaf off the tin. Touch up any bits of white paint that may have come off with the tape or poster putty. Paint a stem onto the leaf with red paint.

6. Cut six lengths of red crepe paper, each about 40 cm (16 in) long. Hot glue the crepe paper pieces around the inside of the tin's bottom.

7. Cut a 35-cm (14-in) length of string. Tape the string ends to the top inside edge of the tin to make a hanger. Then hang your windsock outdoors!

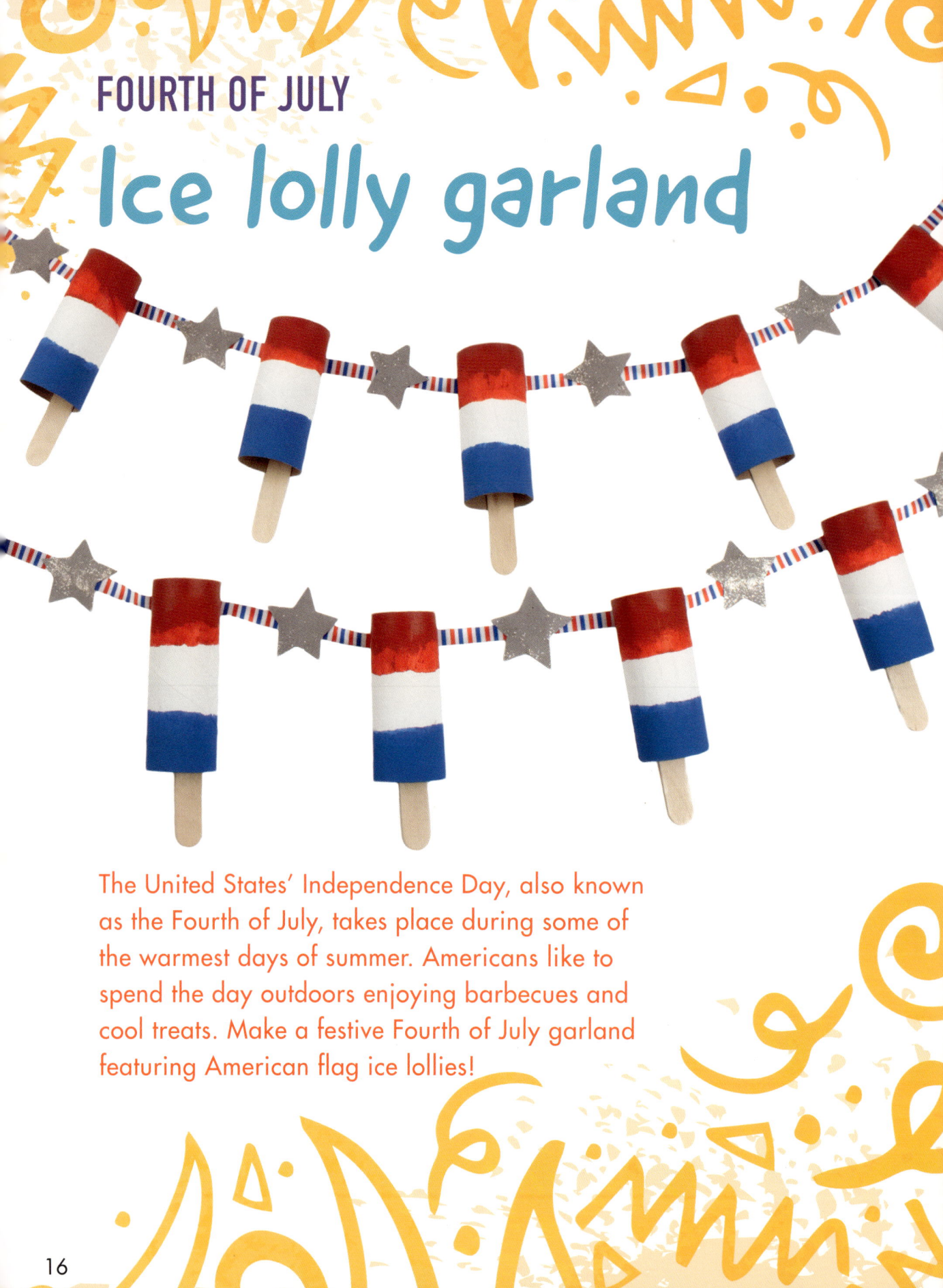

FOURTH OF JULY
Ice lolly garland

The United States' Independence Day, also known as the Fourth of July, takes place during some of the warmest days of summer. Americans like to spend the day outdoors enjoying barbecues and cool treats. Make a festive Fourth of July garland featuring American flag ice lollies!

What you need

- 12 to 18 small, empty cardboard tubes
- paint (white, red, blue) and paintbrushes
- scissors
- hot glue gun
- craft sticks
- ribbon
- ruler
- coloured card
- glitter paint

What you do

1. Paint the middle third of each cardboard tube white. Let the paint dry.

2. Paint the remaining thirds red and blue. Let the paint dry.

3. Cut the craft sticks in half. Hot glue a craft stick inside the blue section of each roll to create ice lollies.

4. Cut the ribbon to the length you want your garland to be. Arrange the lollies vertically or horizontally along the ribbon, leaving space between them. Leave about 10 cm (4 in) of ribbon free on each end of the garland. Glue down the ice lollies.

5. Cut stars out of card and cover them in glitter paint. Let the paint dry. Glue the stars in the spaces between the ice lollies.

6. Hang your garland by the extra ribbon at each end!

BASTILLE DAY
Fireworks cake toppers

On 14 July 1789, French revolutionaries stormed the Bastille, a military fortress in Paris. The event helped spark the French Revolution. Now 14 July is a day of parades, concerts and fireworks across France. Make your own fireworks to mark Bastille Day!

Fun fact
In France, 14 July is better known as Le Quatorze Juillet (The Fourteenth of July) or La Fête Nationale (National Day).

What you need

- silver, red, and blue cellophane
- ruler
- scissors
- craft knife
- clear tape
- glue stick
- wooden skewers

What you do

1. Cut out three 7.5 × 10-cm (3 × 4-in) rectangles of cellophane, one of each colour.

2. Ask an adult to use a craft knife to cut a fringe into one long side of each rectangle.

3. Tape the three rectangles side by side along their short sides.

4. Spread glue over the non-fringed part of the cellophane. Starting at one end, tightly wrap the cellophane around the top 4 cm (1.5 in) of a wooden skewer. Make sure the fringe is facing upwards. This will create a firework burst!

5. Repeat steps 1 to 4 to make more fireworks skewers.

6. Stick your skewers into Bastille Day cakes and other treats for a burst of colour!

NELSON MANDELA INTERNATIONAL DAY

Mandela mosaic

Nelson Mandela was a human rights activist. Beginning in the 1940s, he fought to end racial segregation and discrimination in South Africa. In 1994, he was elected president of South Africa. Mandela's legacy is celebrated every year on his birthday, 18 July. Create a mosaic in honour of this change-maker!

What you need

- cardboard
- ruler
- craft knife
- paint (white, red, green, blue, yellow, black) and paintbrushes
- scissors
- pencil
- reference image of South African flag
- craft glue

What you do

1. Have an adult help you cut out a 30 × 25-cm (12 × 10-in) piece of cardboard using a craft knife. Paint the cardboard white and let it dry.

2. Paint other pieces of cardboard red, green, blue, white, yellow and black. Let the paint dry.

3. Use scissors to cut the painted cardboard from step 2 into small square tiles, about 1.5 × 1.5 cm (½ × ½ inch).

4. In pencil, draw a large heart onto the white cardboard canvas from step 1. Sketch the bands of the South African flag in the heart. Outline the heart in black paint. Let it dry.

5. Use a paintbrush to spread craft glue over a small section of the flag's centre band. Lay green cardboard tiles on the glue. Keep filling in the band one section at a time. Trim the tiles as needed to

fill small gaps. It's okay to leave a bit of space around each tile.

6. Repeat step 5 to fill in the white, yellow, black, and blue bands of the flag.

7. Paint a layer of glue over the tiles once the heart is filled in. Let the glue dry. Then display your mosaic in honour of Nelson Mandela!

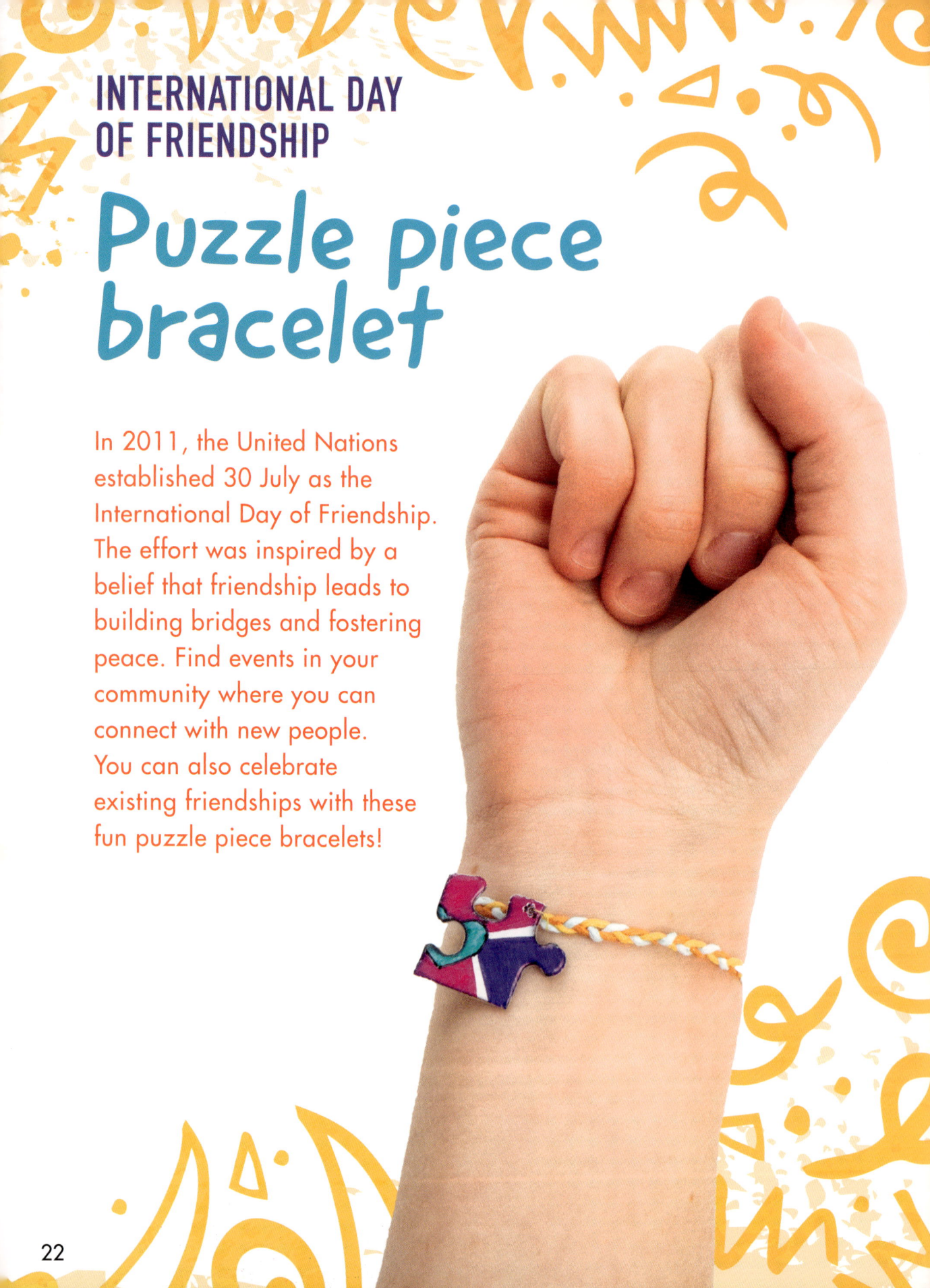

INTERNATIONAL DAY OF FRIENDSHIP

Puzzle piece bracelet

In 2011, the United Nations established 30 July as the International Day of Friendship. The effort was inspired by a belief that friendship leads to building bridges and fostering peace. Find events in your community where you can connect with new people. You can also celebrate existing friendships with these fun puzzle piece bracelets!

What you need

- 2 puzzle pieces that fit together
- paint pen or acrylic paint and paintbrush
- permanent marker pens
- push pin
- sewing thread
- ruler
- string
- scissors

What you do

1. Paint the puzzle pieces and let them dry.

2. Use permanent markers to draw a design across both puzzle pieces.

3. Use a push pin to poke a hole near an edge of each puzzle piece.

4. Cut a 25-cm (10-in) piece of sewing thread for each puzzle piece. Tie the thread through the holes in the puzzle pieces. Knot the thread three times.

5. Cut three 30-cm (12-in) pieces of string. Knot them all together at one end. Plait the strings by crossing the left string over the middle string and then the right string over the middle string in a repeating pattern. Knot the other end. Repeat to make a second string bracelet.

6. Tie each puzzle piece to a bracelet using the thread. Give one bracelet to your friend. You keep the other!

LUGHNASADH
Corn husk doll

Lughnasadh is a Gaelic festival celebrating the start of harvest season. It is also known as Lammas. People celebrate the 1 August holiday by baking bread, gathering for meals and making corn husk dolls. These dolls are easy to make using corn husks, string and felt!

What you need

- corn husks (you can pull husks off fresh corn or buy them online)
- string
- scissors
- felt
- ruler
- hot glue gun

What you do

1. Layer four corn husks on top of each other. Gather them along a short end and tie them together with string.

2. Flip the top two layers over the string knot. Gather the husks around the hidden knot and tie them again to form a head.

3. Roll up another husk and tie it at both ends. Slip the rolled husk underneath the top two layers of the husk doll to form arms. Tie the husk layers beneath the arms to form the doll's waist.

4. Cut a 23 × 7.5-cm (9 × 3-in) rectangle out of felt. Fold it in half and cut a half circle into the fold.

5. Place the doll's head through the hole. Use a strip of felt to tie the felt tunic around the doll's waist.

6. Use felt to create more accessories for your doll, such as a bonnet. Use hot glue to attach the accessories as needed. Then play with your doll!

HUNGRY GHOST FESTIVAL

Lucky orange slices

The Hungry Ghost Festival takes place during the seventh month of the lunar calendar. According to Chinese tradition, the souls of the dead are released into the world of the living during this time. To keep the spirits happy, people leave offerings of oranges, tea and more. Make your own hungry ghost offering in the form of a dried-orange garland!

Fun fact

The Hungry Ghost Festival is known as Zhong Yuan Jie in Chinese.

What you need

- 2 unpeeled oranges
- knife
- kitchen roll
- baking tray
- greaseproof paper
- oven
- toothpick
- ruler
- string
- scissors
- duct tape

What you do

1. Ask an adult to cut the oranges into slices 0.5 cm (¼-in) thick. Use kitchen roll to soak up the juice from each slice.

2. Line a baking tray with greaseproof paper. Lay the orange slices in a single layer on the paper.

3. Bake the orange slices at 120 degrees Celsius (250 degrees Fahrenheit) for one hour and 15 minutes. Ask an adult to help you flip the orange slices. Then bake them for another hour and 15 minutes. Let the slices cool.

4. Use a toothpick to poke two holes about 2.5 cm (1 in) apart in each dried orange slice.

5. Cut a 90-cm (36-inch) length of string. Tie several knots at one end to form one large knot. Wrap the other end in duct tape.

6. Thread the duct-taped end of string through the two holes of

an orange slice. Move the orange slice down the string until it reaches the knot.

7. Repeat step 6 to thread the rest of the orange slices.

8. Knot the string above the last orange slice. Tie a loop and cut off any remaining string. Then hang your garland from the loop!

27

JUNETEENTH
Hibiscus flower punch topper

Juneteenth celebrates the end of enslavement in the United States. Juneteenth gatherings often feature red food and drinks. The colour symbolizes blood shed by enslaved Africans. It also represents the hibiscus plant native to West Africa. Sip a red drink from a hibiscus flower straw in honour of Juneteenth!

What you need

- red card
- ruler
- scissors
- pencil
- glue stick
- yellow crepe paper
- paper or plastic drinking straw
- small elastic band

What you do

1. Cut a 10 × 10-cm (4 × 4-inch) square of red card.

2. Fold the square from one corner to the opposite corner, forming a triangle.

3. Fold the triangle from one corner to the opposite corner, making a smaller triangle.

4. Repeat step 3 to make the triangle even smaller.

5. Cut the folded triangle into a petal shape. Make sure you leave the creased side of the triangle intact as you cut.

6. Unfold the petal shape to reveal a flower.

7. Wrap the tip of each flower petal around a pencil to make the petals curl downwards.

8. Make a cut between two petals to the centre of the flower. Then overlap the two petals and glue them together.

9. Cut a strip of yellow crepe paper that is 20 cm (8 in) long. Make small cuts into one of the long sides to make a fringe.

10. Dab glue on the non-fringed long side of the paper strip. Wrap the strip in a tight spiral around the straw about 5 cm (2 in) from the top. Make sure the fringe points up. Use glue to secure the other end of the strip to the straw.

11. Cut the point off the underside of your flower to create a small hole.

12. Push the bottom of the straw through the hole in the flower. Bring the flower up to the base of the fringe. If the flower is loose, wrap a small rubber band around the straw below the flower to keep the flower in place.

13. Drop your straw into a red drink and enjoy!

Fun fact

Hibiscus flowers are used to make a variety of drinks. Bissap is a hibiscus drink popular in the West African country Senegal.

FIND OUT MORE

BOOKS

10-Minute Crafty Projects (10-Minute Makers), Elsie Olson (Raintree, 2022)

Celebrations Around the World (Customs Around the World), Wil Mara (Raintree, 2021)

Nature Art (Awesome Art), Jeanette Ryall (Raintree, 2021)

WEBSITES

learnenglishkids.britishcouncil.org/category/topics/festivals-and-celebrations
Find out about different world festivals and celebrations as well as some craft activities on this website.

www.bbc.co.uk/cbbc/curations/bp-arts-and-crafts-collection
CBBC has lots of craft ideas you can make.

ABOUT THE AUTHOR

Megan Borgert-Spaniol is an author and editor of children's media. When she isn't writing or reading, she enjoys doing yoga, eating croissants and making homemade pizzas. Megan lives in Minneapolis, Minnesota, USA, with a tall, goofy man and a small, chatty cat.